LETS CREATE ART

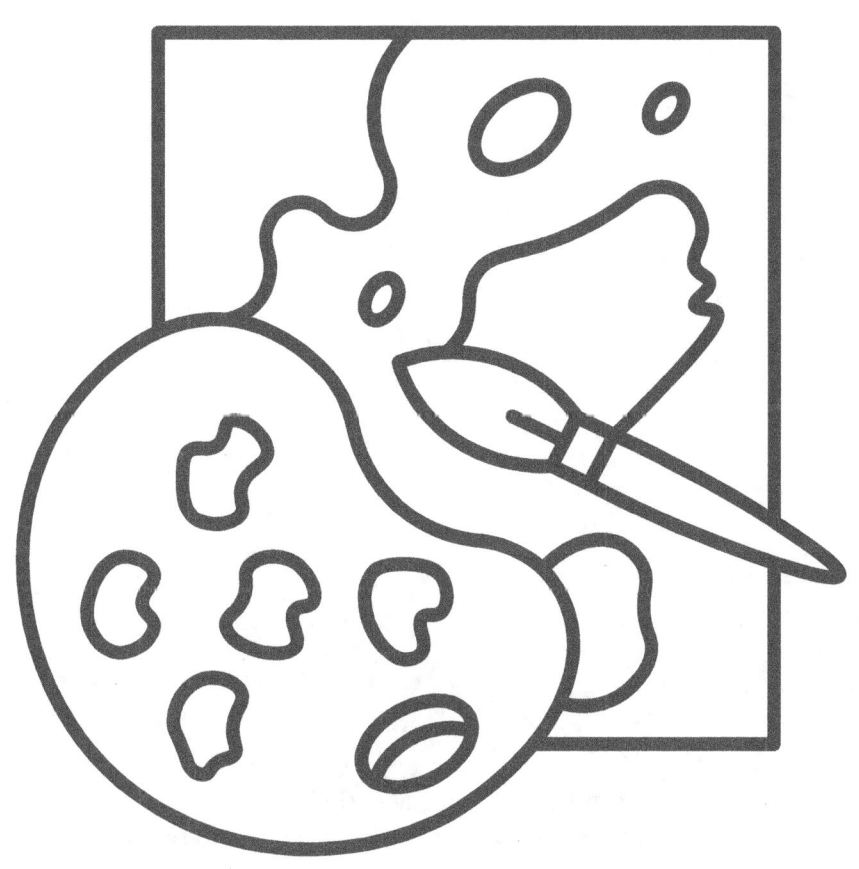

Instructions

1. Follow the prompts.
2. Have fun.
3. There's no right or wrong way.
4. Don't be afraid of the blank page.
5. Do them in any order.
6. Use the blank pages too.

Write your name in any style

....

....

....

....

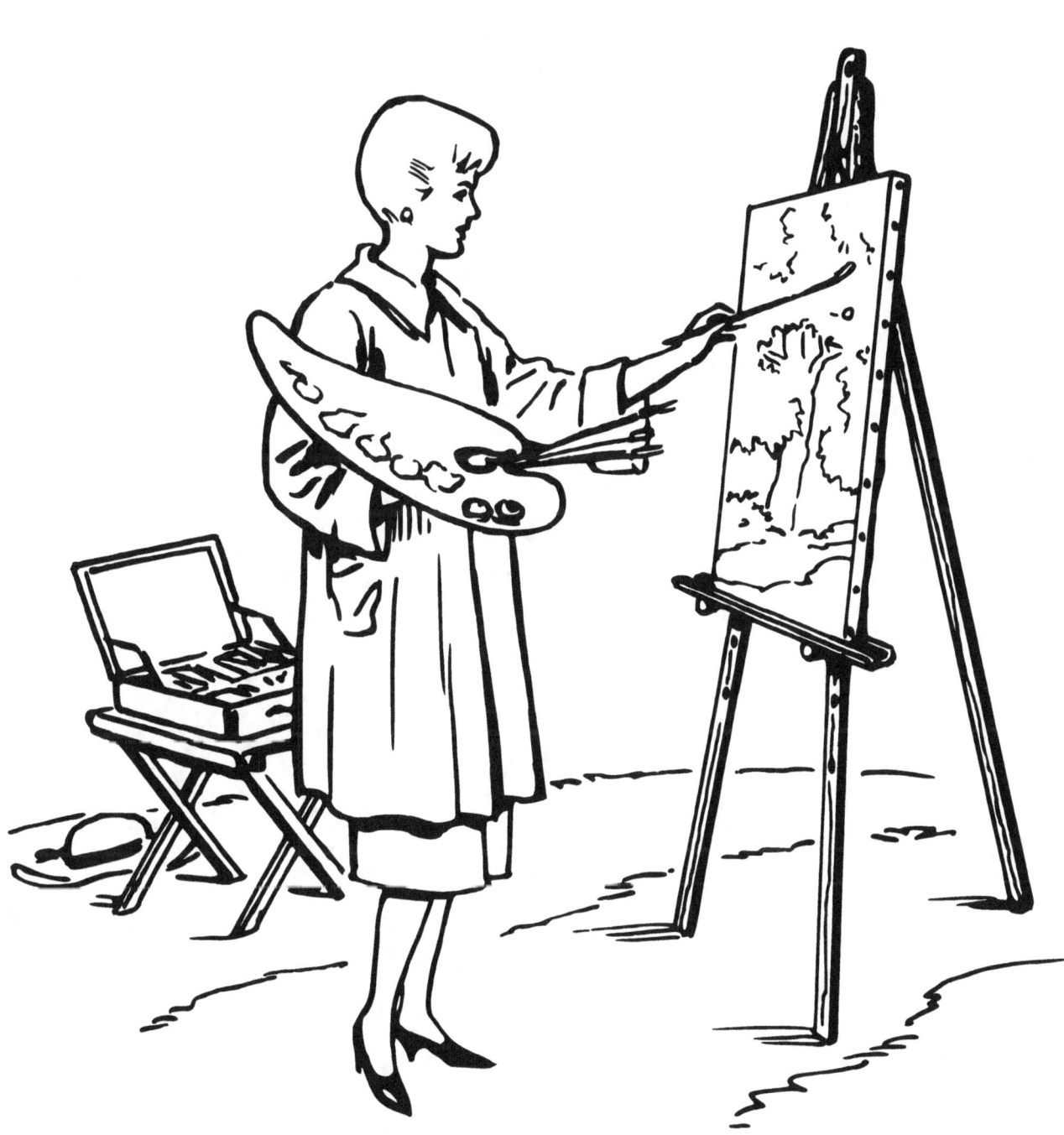

face your fear of the first blank page

Make a character using thumbprints

FILL THIS PAGE WITH COLOUR

Fill the page with squiggles

Cold

Colour Me

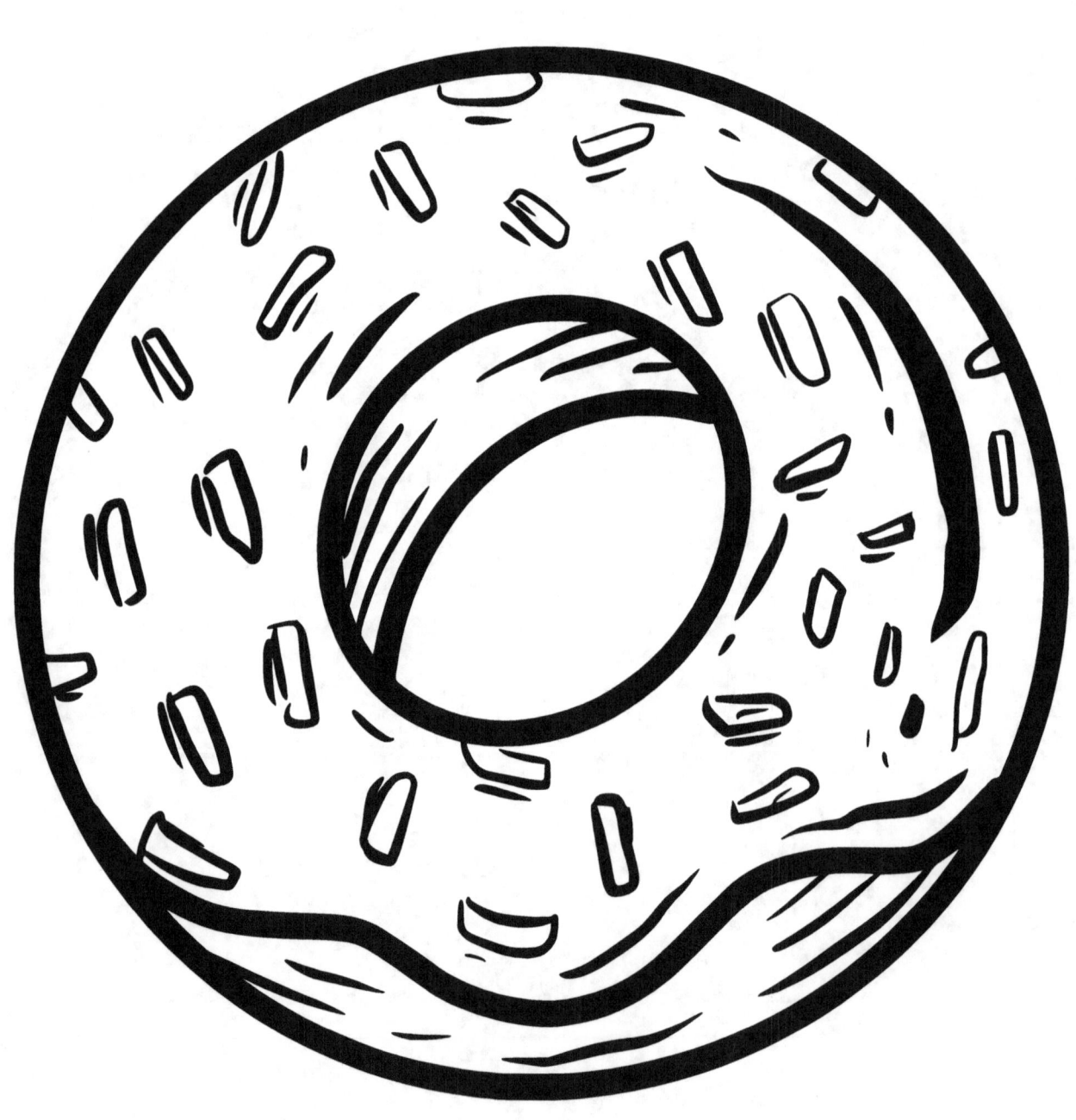

Hot

Random objects

Using pens, pencils or paints

Be Inspired

Swatch Page

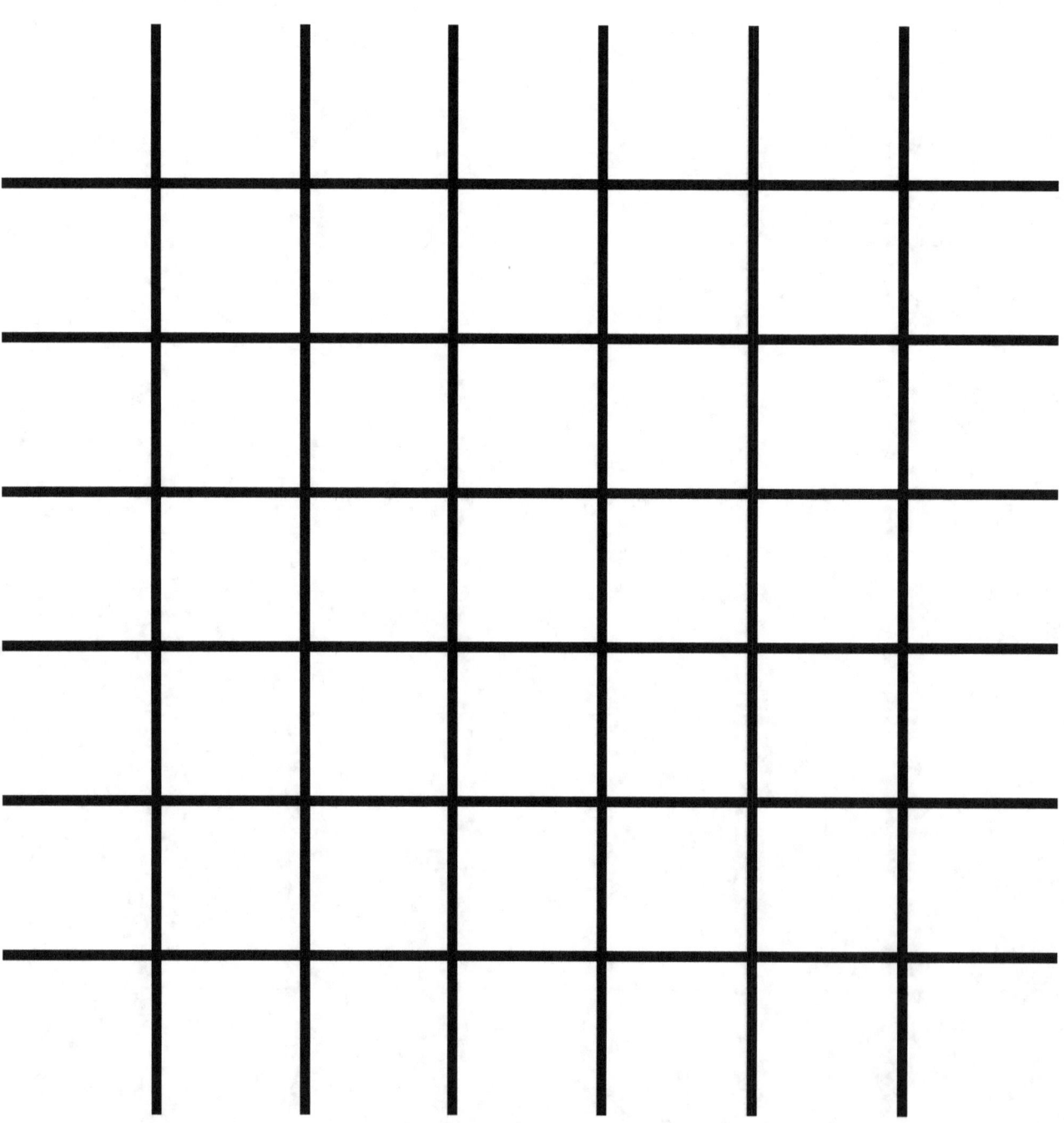

Stick leaves here

Draw or paint the leaf

Paint or draw using your mouth

GRAFFITI

This page

Fill this page with things beginning with any letter From the alphabet

Give this book too an elderly relative or Friend to draw on these pages

Winter

SPLODGE PAINT

How do you Feel

Draw how you feel

Draw or Paint your Pet

Monochrome
Use one colour

Draw your Favourite meal

Fill the page with yellow things

Draw or Paint with a twig

Everyday
objects
Paint or draw

Love to doodle

One word

Fill these pages
with one word

Do an ugly drawing

Beauty

water

Magical

Flower

Draw or paint a
flower

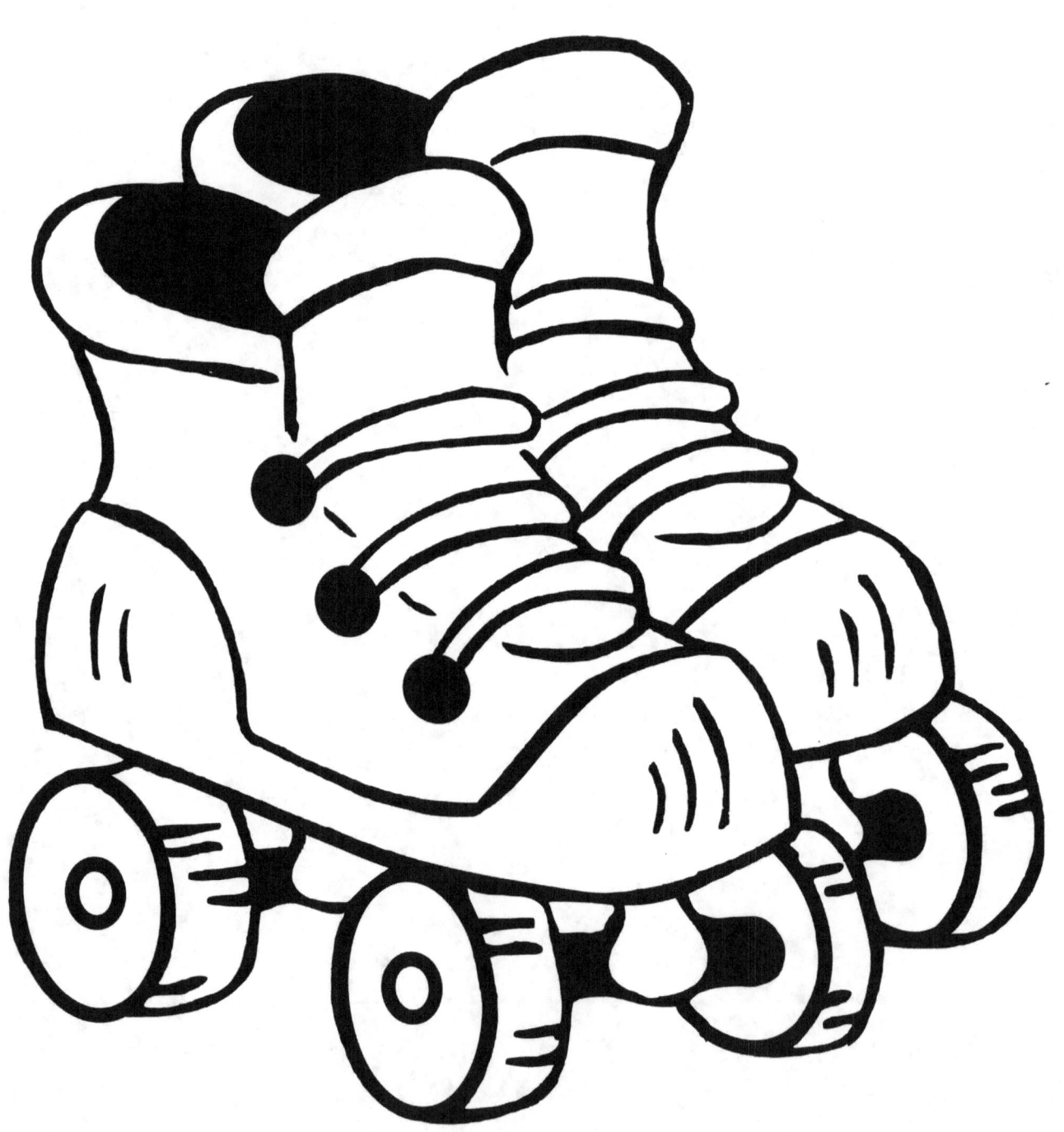

Time goes by
show time passing by

Draw around your hand

Be happy

Fear

Draw around your Feet

Pencil rubbings
Using graphite or coloured pencils

Friendship

Easter

Messy
Make a mess

Draw or colour the edges of the book

The weather

Draw a member of your Family

Sound

Draw insects

Draw or paint a Food character

Give your Food arms, legs etc.

spring

Crying

Sandwich

Fill the page with art supplies

Draw some thing around your house

Design a board game

Halloween

Bright

Draw inside Front and back cover

Fill these pages with swirls

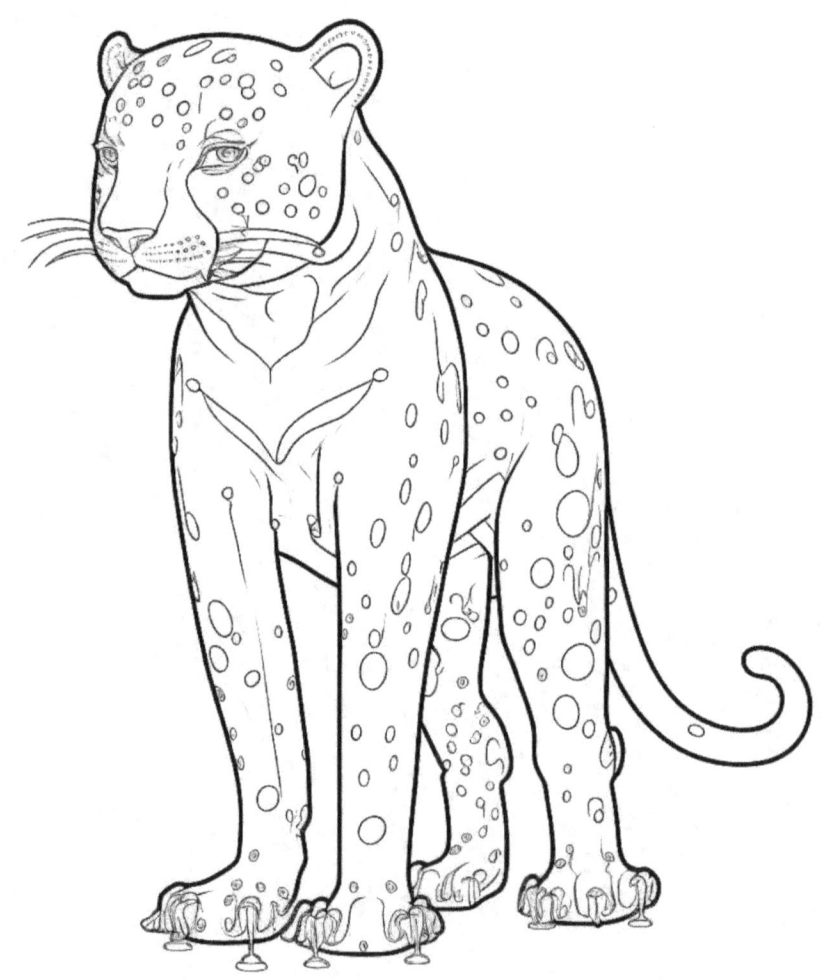

My favourite colour

My least favourite colour

Make your mark

Draw your Favourite animal

Summer

Design a t-shirt

Use stencils

Draw a character
tv, cartoon,movie etc

Self Portrait

Valentine

Objects in pocket or bag

draw the items

Autumn

Draw something
in the colour black
using pen, pencil
etc

Party

Draw or paint fruit or vegetables

Christmas

Create a logo

Colour Me

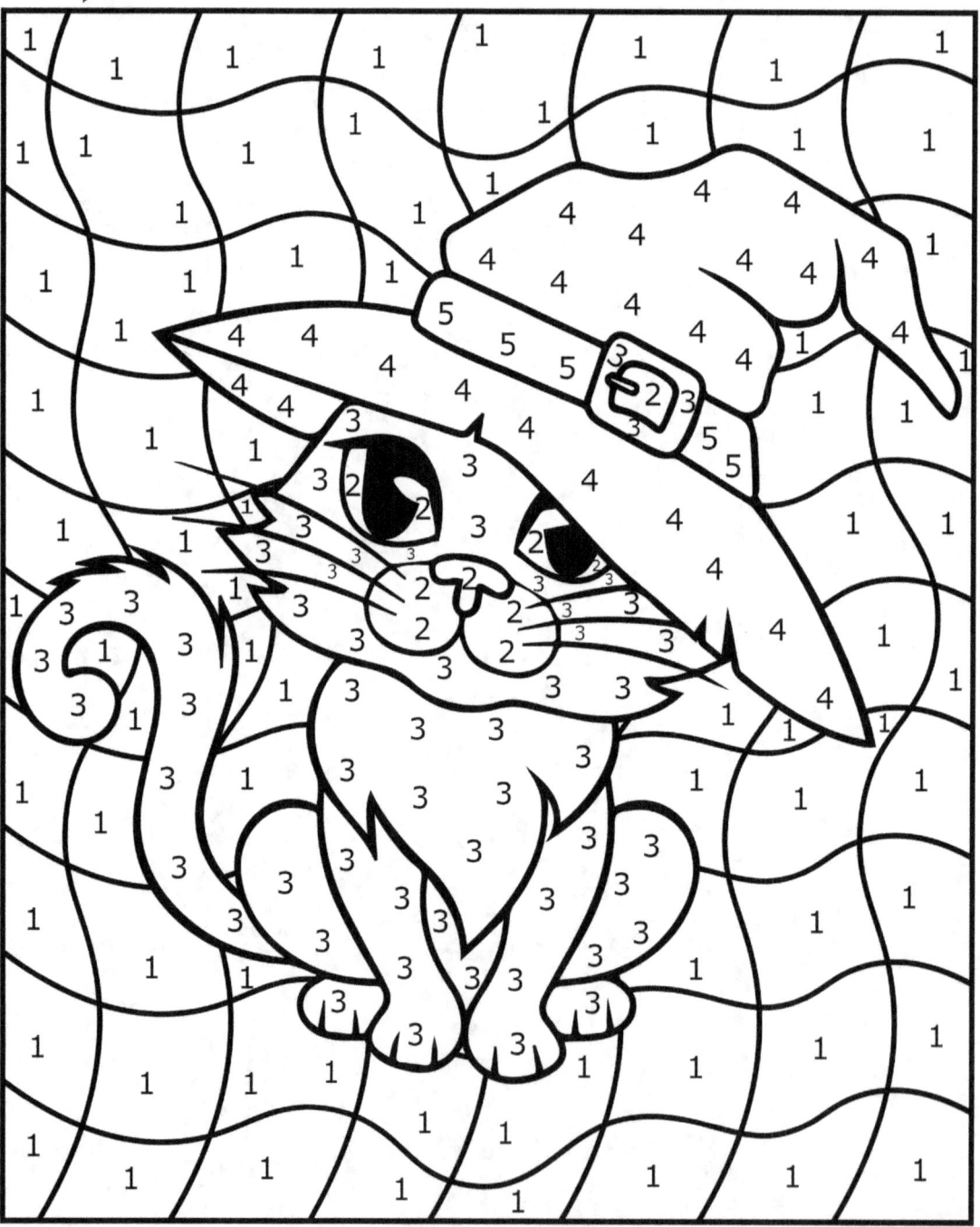

1=DarkGreen 2=Red 3=DimGray 4=Orange
5=Black

www.ingramcontent.com/pod-product-compliance
Lightning Source LLC
Chambersburg PA
CBHW082213290526
45794CB00009B/3523